LEON FURZE

STARTING HIGH SCHOOL

Confidently Navigate The School Experience

Copyright © Leon Furze 2023

All rights reserved. No part of this book may be reproduced or transmitted in any form or by any means, electronic or mechanical, including photocopying, recording or by any information storage and retrieval system, without prior permission in writing from the publisher.

Published in 2023

Published by Amba Press
Melbourne, Australia
www.ambapress.com.au

Cover designer – Tess McCabe
Editor – Beth Browne

ISBN: 9781922607621 (pbk)
ISBN: 9781922607638 (ebk)

A catalogue record for this book is available from the National Library of Australia.

Table of Contents

Chapter 1:	Getting ready for a new beginning	4
Chapter 2:	Making friends and fitting in (or not!)	10
Chapter 3:	Navigating the classroom and homework	18
Chapter 4:	Dealing with bullies and standing up for yourself	25
Chapter 5:	Finding your passion and getting involved	34
Chapter 6:	Preparing for tests and exams	40
Chapter 7:	Balancing academic and extracurricular activities	46
Chapter 8:	Understanding and managing stress	54
Chapter 9:	Mental health matters: understanding and taking care of yourself	60
Chapter 10:	Being yourself: embracing your unique identity	68
Chapter 11:	Looking to the future: setting goals and dreaming big	74
Chapter 12:	Devices and digital technologies	80
Chapter 13:	Growing and learning: how to embrace change	88
Conclusion		94

Chapter 1

Getting ready for a new beginning

Getting ready for a new beginning

In this chapter, we will be discussing the importance of setting goals and having a positive attitude, understanding and managing expectations, and building a support network. By following the advice and tips in this chapter, you will be better prepared for your transition to secondary school and be able to navigate the challenges that come with it.

Tips for preparing for the transition to secondary school

The transition from primary to secondary school can be a big step, and it's natural to feel a mix of excitement and nerves. But don't worry, this book is here to help guide you through the process and make it as smooth as possible. Inside, you will find valuable information and tips for before, during and after your transition to secondary school. Whether you're in Year 5, Year 6 or about to start secondary school, this book is a great resource that will help you prepare for the changes ahead and give you the confidence you need to succeed. Remember, you are not alone in this journey and I am here to support you every step of the way.

The importance of setting goals and having a positive attitude

One of the best ways to prepare for your transition to secondary school is by setting some goals for yourself. These goals can help you focus on what you want to achieve and give you a sense of direction during this time of change. In this book, we will be discussing goal-setting in more detail later. But for now, let's start with some simple goals for your first few days and weeks of secondary school. Here are a few questions to help you get started:

- What are some things you want to achieve during your first week of secondary school?
- What are some new experiences you want to try?
- How do you want to make new friends?
- What are some things you want to learn during your first term?

Understanding and managing expectations

Great job setting your goals! Another important step in preparing for secondary school is having a clear set of expectations. Everyone's experience of secondary school is different, and it can be helpful to have a clear understanding of what to expect. Maybe you have an older sibling or friends who are in secondary school and have shared their experiences with you. Or maybe you have no idea what to expect. Regardless of your current understanding, having clear expectations can help you feel more prepared and confident as you start secondary school. To help you write down your expectations, consider the following prompts:

- What are your expectations of the school environment?
- What are your expectations of the teachers?
- What are your expectations of the curriculum and classes?
- What are your expectations of the students?

Now that you've got some expectations written down, you should check them to see if anything is unrealistic. Managing your expectations means not being too *pessimistic* (looking on the bad side). It can also mean not getting carried away and being too *optimistic*. Secondary school is like everything else – it has its ups and downs!

Building a support network

Identifying your support network before starting your transition to secondary school can be really helpful. Your support network is made up of people who can offer you guidance, advice and encouragement throughout your journey.

Some people who may be part of your support network include:

- family members, such as parents, siblings or grandparents
- friends and classmates
- teachers and school counsellors
- coaches or mentors.

It's also important to consider other supports such as:

- access to mental health services
- access to online resources and support groups.

Having a strong support network can provide you with the emotional and practical support you need to navigate the challenges of secondary school. Make sure to communicate and build relationships with the people in your support network, and don't hesitate to reach out to them when you need help or advice.

Chapter 2

Making friends and fitting in (or not!)

Strategies for making new friends

Making new friends can be a bit of a challenge, especially when you're starting secondary school. But don't worry, there are things you can do to make it easier. Here are a few tips to help you make new friends:

1. **Join clubs or groups:** Joining a club or group that interests you is a great way to meet new people who share your interests. It could be a sports team, a drama club or even a school band.

2. **Be yourself:** Don't be afraid to be yourself. People are more likely to be your friend if they like you for who you are.

3. **Listen more than you talk:** When you first meet someone, try to listen more than you talk. This will show that you're interested in what they have to say and that you value their thoughts.

4. **Don't be afraid to take the initiative:** Sometimes, you may need to be the one to initiate a conversation or invite someone to hang out. It may be a bit scary, but taking the initiative can be a great way to make new friends.

5. **Keep in touch:** If you have friends from primary school, make sure to keep in touch with them. It's important to nurture old friendships as well as make new ones.

6. **Be open to different types of people:** Try to get to know people from different backgrounds, cultures and interests. You never know, you might find a friend in the most unexpected places.

Remember, making friends takes time and patience. Be yourself and don't be discouraged if it takes a while to find the right people. And most importantly, don't be afraid to put yourself out there and take the initiative.

Understanding and dealing with social anxiety

Social anxiety is a common concern for many students as they transition to secondary school. It's important to understand that social anxiety is a normal feeling and it's nothing to be ashamed of. Social anxiety is defined as a persistent fear of one or more social or performance situations in which the person is exposed to unfamiliar people or to possible scrutiny by others.

If you are experiencing social anxiety, it can be helpful to try the following strategies:

1. Seek out a school counsellor or therapist for support. They can help you learn coping strategies to manage your anxiety.

2. Practise deep breathing and other relaxation techniques before social situations.

3. Try to challenge negative thoughts and beliefs about yourself and social situations.

4. Consider joining a support group for teens with social anxiety.

5. Gradually expose yourself to social situations, starting with small, low-pressure situations and gradually working your way up to bigger, more challenging situations.

6. Practise positive self-talk and focus on your strengths and accomplishments.

7. Seek out supportive friends and family members who can provide emotional support and encouragement.

It's important to remember that social anxiety can be overcome with time, patience and support. Don't be afraid to ask for help, and remember that you are not alone.

The importance of being true to yourself

It's important to remember that making friends doesn't mean you have to change who you are or lose sight of your individuality. You should never feel pressure to pretend to be someone else or follow the crowd just to fit in. Being true to yourself is much more important than fitting in with a certain group or clique.

Here are a few tips to help you stay true to yourself while making friends:

- **Be yourself:** People are more likely to be your friend if they like you for who you are, so don't be afraid to be yourself.

- **Follow your interests:** Join clubs or groups that align with your interests. This way, you'll meet like-minded individuals who share similar hobbies and interests.

- **Don't compare yourself to others:** It's easy to feel pressure to conform to certain standards or expectations, but remember that everyone is unique and has their own strengths and weaknesses.

- **Speak up:** Share your thoughts and opinions, and don't be afraid to disagree with others when necessary.

- **Don't compromise your values:** Stay true to your beliefs and values, even if they differ from those of your friends.

- **Surround yourself with positive people:** Look for friends who respect and accept you for who you are and avoid those who pressure you to change.

Remember, it's important to be true to yourself and not lose sight of who you are in the process of making friends. Surround yourself with people who accept and respect you for who you are, and don't be afraid to be different.

How to deal with rejection and exclusion

Everyone experiences feelings of rejection and exclusion at some point in their lives. It's normal to feel left out or rejected, especially during the transition to secondary school. Navigating new social situations and making new friends can be difficult.

It's important to remember that rejection is not a reflection of your worth. Just because someone doesn't want to be friends with you, doesn't mean that you're not good enough or that there's something wrong with you. Sometimes rejection has nothing to do with you and is a result of the other person's issues or circumstances.

If you're feeling rejected or excluded, it can be helpful to seek support from a trusted friend or family member. They can offer a fresh perspective and provide emotional support. Additionally, finding other ways to connect with people who share your interests can be a great way to build new friendships.

Practising self-care is also important. Engage in activities that make you feel good and remind yourself of your strengths and accomplishments. Keeping things in perspective is important. Remember that rejection and exclusion are not the end of the world and that there will be many opportunities to connect with others in the future.

It's important to remember that rejection is not the end. Keep an open mind and don't give up on the idea of making new friends. You will find the right people at the right time. Don't let rejection or exclusion define you, and always remember that you are worthy and deserving of friendship.

Chapter 3

Navigating the classroom and homework

Tips for staying organised and managing time

When you start secondary school, one of the biggest changes you'll notice is how different your daily schedule is compared to primary school. In most Australian secondary schools, the day is divided into five or six periods where you rotate through different subjects. This is different from primary school, where you might have had specific blocks of time for subjects like literacy or numeracy and regular days of the week for subjects like art or sports. In secondary school, these subjects might be mixed up and spread out over a week or even two weeks.

It can be a bit overwhelming at first, but don't worry! You will soon get used to the new schedule. It's helpful to make a timetable for yourself to keep track of when your classes are and what subjects you have on what days.

Another important thing to know is that in secondary school you might have different teachers for each subject. This means that you may have a different teacher for mathematics, science, English and so on. This is different from primary school, where you might have had one teacher for most of the day. It can be a bit scary at first, but you will soon get to know your new teachers and they will help you to feel comfortable.

In secondary school, you will also have a lot more homework and assignments to do than you did in primary school, so it's important to be organised and to manage your time well. Make sure to plan your study time and work on your assignments in a quiet place where you won't be distracted.

Strategies for managing your new timetable

Here are a few strategies to help manage your timetable:

1. **Make a timetable for yourself:** Keep track of when your classes are and what subjects you have on what days. This will help you stay organised and on top of your work. Your teacher might give you a planner or timetable template, but it may help to make your own.

2. **Get to know your teachers:** Introduce yourself to your new teachers and ask for their help if you need it. They are there to support you and will be happy to help you feel comfortable in their class.

3. **Manage your time effectively:** With more homework and assignments to do, it's important to manage your time well. Plan your study time and work on your assignments in a quiet place where you won't be distracted.

4. **Prioritise your tasks:** Make a to-do list and prioritise the most important tasks first. This will help you stay focused and avoid feeling overwhelmed.

5. **Seek help if needed:** If you are struggling to manage your timetable or are feeling overwhelmed, don't hesitate to seek help from your teachers, school counsellor or parents. They are there to support you and will be happy to help you find solutions.

How to study effectively

As you enter secondary school, you'll find that the pace and difficulty of some of your studies increases. That's perfectly normal and hopefully not too overwhelming as you begin Year 7. Here are a few ways you can learn to study effectively both in and out of school which can help you avoid becoming overwhelmed:

- **Prioritise your studies:** Make a schedule or to-do list of all the tasks you need to complete and prioritise the most important ones first.

- **Create a study environment:** Find a quiet and comfortable place to study where you won't be easily distracted.

- **Take breaks:** Take regular breaks to recharge and avoid burnout. Move around, listen to music or read a book to clear your mind.

- **Practise time management:** Use a timer or an app to manage your time effectively and make sure you're not procrastinating.

- **Stay organised:** Keep track of important dates, assignments and due dates in a planner or calendar.

- **Seek help if needed:** If you are struggling to understand a concept or topic, don't hesitate to seek help from your teachers, school counsellor or parents. They are there to support you and will be happy to help you find solutions.

- **Practise active listening and note-taking:** Pay attention during class, take notes and review them later, and ask questions if you don't understand something.

- **Practise regularly:** Practice makes perfect. The more you practise, the more you'll understand the material and the easier it will be to remember.

By following these strategies, you will be able to manage your studies effectively, stay organised and avoid becoming overwhelmed. Remember to take it one step at a time, and don't hesitate to ask for help if you need it.

How to ask for help if needed

Just because you're entering an unfamiliar environment doesn't mean you have to go it alone. If you're finding it hard to juggle your classwork and homework, don't be afraid to ask for help. Here are a few ways to ask for help when you need it:

1. **Talk to your teachers:** Your teachers are there to help you succeed and understand the material. If you're struggling with a concept or assignment, don't be afraid to ask for extra help during class or after class.

2. **Seek out a tutor:** If you're having trouble keeping up with your classwork, consider finding a tutor who can give you extra help and support.

3. **Ask for help from your school counsellor:** Your school counsellor can provide you with guidance and resources to help you manage your workload and stay on track.

4. **Talk to your parents or guardians:** Your parents or guardians can provide you with emotional support and may be able to help you with your homework or assignments.

5. **Join a study group:** Joining a study group can be a great way to get extra help and support. You can share notes, study together and help each other understand the material.

6. **Ask for help from a teacher's assistant or student mentor:** Some schools have teacher's assistants or student mentors who can provide extra help and support to students.

7. **Use safe online resources:** There are many online resources such as websites, videos and forums that can help you with your studies. A teacher or trusted adult can point you to safe online resources.

Chapter 4

Dealing with bullies and standing up for yourself

Understanding the different types of bullying

Bullying is a serious problem that can have harmful effects on those who experience it. It can take many forms, including physical, verbal and social bullying.

Physical bullying includes behaviours that involve physical contact and are intended to harm or intimidate someone. Examples of physical bullying include fighting, pushing or hitting someone. Physical bullying can be especially dangerous because it can cause physical injuries and can also lead to long-term physical and emotional consequences for the person being bullied.

Verbal bullying involves using words to hurt or intimidate someone. This can include teasing or name-calling and can be done in person or online. Verbal bullying can be just as harmful as physical bullying, as it can cause emotional pain and damage to a person's self-esteem.

Social bullying involves excluding someone from social activities or spreading rumours about them. This can include things like excluding someone from a group or spreading false information about them to damage their reputation. Social bullying can be particularly harmful because it can cause a person to feel isolated and ostracised.

Online bullying, also known as cyberbullying, involves using social media or other forms of electronic communication to bully someone. This can include sending harassing messages or spreading rumours online. Online bullying can be especially harmful because it can be done anonymously and it can reach a wide audience very quickly. It can also be difficult to escape, as the person being bullied may feel like they are constantly being targeted, even when they are not online.

How to recognise bullying

It is important to be able to recognise the signs of bullying in your friends and family. Here are some of the most common signs to look out for if a person if being bullied:

1. **Saying they feel hopeless or empty:** This could include statements such as "I don't see the point in anything", "I don't have a future", or "I don't care about anything".

2. **Outbursts of anger and crying for no obvious reason:** This could involve sudden and unexpected displays of anger or crying that seem to come out of nowhere and are not connected to a specific event or situation.

3. **Losing interest in activities that used to bring them joy:** This could involve no longer wanting to participate in hobbies, sports or other activities that the person previously enjoyed.

4. **Reacting with extreme anger or frustration to small problems:** This could involve overreacting to minor issues or becoming easily agitated or frustrated in situations that would normally not cause such a strong response.

5. **Feeling bad about themselves, guilty and worthless:** This could involve negative self-talk, feeling like they are a burden to others or feeling like they do not have value or worth.

If someone you know is exhibiting the above signs, it is important to take them seriously and offer support to the person.

Bullying, self-confidence and self-esteem

Bullying can have a negative impact on your self-esteem and confidence. When someone is bullied, they may feel embarrassed, ashamed or unworthy. They may also feel helpless and lack confidence in their ability to stand up for themselves or to stop the bullying from happening. These negative feelings can lead to a decline in self-esteem and confidence.

It's important to understand that self-esteem and confidence are closely related. Self-esteem refers to how much you value and respect yourself, while confidence refers to your belief in your abilities and capacity to achieve your goals. When someone experiences bullying, it can cause them to doubt their worth and abilities, leading to a decline in both self-esteem and confidence.

It's important to take active steps to improve your self-esteem and confidence, especially when dealing with bullying. Surrounding yourself with positive and supportive people, engaging in activities that you enjoy and practising self-care can all help boost your self-esteem and confidence. It's also important to remember that you are not alone and that there are people who care about you and want to help.

Strategies for standing up for yourself and others

Standing up to bullies can be tough, but it is important to be able to make yourself heard. This is true whether you are the person being bullied or you are supporting a friend or loved one.

Here are five ways you can stand up to bullies and promote more positive social interactions:

1. **Use "I" statements to express your feelings and boundaries:** Instead of saying "You're wrong", try saying "I feel hurt when you say that". This helps to express your own feelings and boundaries without being confrontational.

2. **Practise assertive communication:** Be clear and direct in expressing your needs and boundaries. It's okay to say no and to set limits on how you want to be treated.

3. **Use humour to defuse a tense situation:** If a bully is trying to get a rise out of you, try using humour to defuse the situation. This can take the wind out of their sails and show that you are not going to be an easy target.

4. **Seek support from trusted adults or friends:** It can be helpful to have someone to talk to and to help you come up with strategies for dealing with the bully.

5. **Take care of yourself:** It's important to take care of your own wellbeing and to engage in activities that help you to feel good about yourself. This can give you the confidence and resilience you need to stand up to bullies.

Chapter 5

Finding your passion and getting involved

How to explore your interests and passions

Maybe you'll be starting secondary school with a clear idea of your passions and interests. Or perhaps you still haven't found things that you really love. Either way, starting secondary school is a great opportunity to explore your interests and passions. For example, you might want to try out new sports, clubs or activities that are available at your school. Here are a few suggestions to help you explore your interests and passions:

1. **Take advantage of the opportunities offered by your school:** Many secondary schools offer a wide range of extracurricular activities, from sports teams and music ensembles to clubs and societies. Take the time to explore the options available to you and consider trying something new.

2. **Talk to your teachers:** Your teachers can provide valuable guidance and advice on how to explore your interests and passions. They may also be able to connect you with resources or opportunities that can help you pursue your interests.

3. **Get involved in your community:** There are many opportunities to explore your interests and passions outside of school. Look for volunteer or community service opportunities, clubs and organisations in your area that align with your interests.

4. **Try different activities:** Give yourself the chance to try different activities and hobbies until you find something that you truly enjoy.

The benefits of extracurricular activities and clubs

Participating in activities outside of the classroom, such as music, sports, debate clubs and volunteering, is a great way to explore your interests and passions, develop new skills and build your confidence. These activities can also help you make new friends and build strong relationships with your peers. Not only that, but they also have an impact on your overall wellbeing by improving your physical and mental health.

Getting involved in these activities can help you get involved in your school and community and can also make a positive impact on the world around you. They can help you build a sense of self-worth and confidence and provide you with valuable experiences and skills that will serve you well throughout your life. Whether you're looking for a fun and engaging way to spend your time outside of school or wanting to improve your overall wellbeing, consider participating in extracurricular activities.

How to find and join clubs and activities

Here are a few ways to find extracurricular activities in your school and community:

- **Sports:** Sports are the most common extracurricular activity for young people in Australia. Swimming lessons, ice skating lessons, gymnastics and soccer clinics are typically offered to children as early as the toddler and preschool years. Many local recreation departments offer AFL, baseball, lacrosse, hockey, tennis, ultimate frisbee, running and volleyball to secondary school students.

- **Scouts:** Scouting groups are a great choice for anyone who enjoys nature and is willing to try a variety of activities. Scouts learn basic outdoor survival skills, but they are also expected to earn badges in other skills such as cooking, cleaning, arts, finances, goal-setting and personal care.

- **Performing arts:** Theatre and dance are popular extracurricular activities found in almost every community. Many schools and community theatres put on plays and other performances that students can participate in by either trying out or just signing up. Other students who enjoy stagecraft but not performing may help build sets; work on lights, sound and special effects; or make costumes.

- **Visual arts:** If you like to draw, paint or create, you might benefit from joining an art program to learn art techniques and see your creativity flourish.

- **Music:** Band and choir are popular elective courses in many schools. You can also get private lessons or join a community youth orchestra or other music groups.

- **Community service:** Service organisations and not-for-profits are great places to learn about social and humanitarian issues.

You can often find out about these kinds of activities and clubs through your school, at a library or at a community information centre.

How to overcome shyness and self-doubt

Joining clubs and activities can be a great way to meet new people, make friends and explore your interests. However, for some students, the idea of joining a club or activity can be daunting. If you're shy, the thought of meeting new people and trying something new can be overwhelming. But it's important to remember that everyone feels shy sometimes. Just because you're shy doesn't mean you can't join a club or activity. In fact, joining a club or activity can be a great way to overcome shyness.

When you join a club or activity, you're surrounded by people who share your interests. This can make it easier to start a conversation and make friends. You'll also have the opportunity to learn new skills and try new things, which can help to boost your confidence. And as you become more comfortable with the people in the club or activity, you'll find that it becomes easier to talk to them and make friends.

It's also important to remember that most people are understanding and supportive. They won't judge you if you're shy, and they'll be happy to help you feel comfortable. Many clubs and activities have leaders or advisers who can help you get started and answer any questions you may have. So don't let shyness hold you back from joining a club or activity. Give it a try and see how it can help you to overcome shyness and make new friends.

Chapter 6

Preparing for tests and exams

Study strategies and tips for success

Tests and exams are an important part of the school experience. They help to evaluate what you have learned and assess your understanding of the material. Here are some tips to help you prepare for tests and exams:

1. **Set up a study schedule:** Create a study schedule to ensure you have enough time to cover all the material that will be tested. Allocate more time for topics that you find challenging.

2. **Find a study group:** Join a study group or form your own with classmates who are serious about their studies. Studying with others can help you learn from each other and stay motivated.

3. **Take good notes:** Develop a note-taking system that works for you. Use headings, bullet points and diagrams to organise your notes. Your teacher can help you to learn ways of taking good notes.

4. **Use flashcards:** Flashcards are an effective way to memorise important facts, definitions and formulas. Quiz yourself regularly to test your memory. This is especially useful for subjects where you have to learn facts and content.

5. **Practise active learning:** Rather than simply reading through your notes, actively engage with the material by asking questions, making connections and applying what you've learned.

How to manage test anxiety

One effective way to manage test anxiety is to practise relaxation techniques. Deep breathing, visualisation and guided meditation can all help to calm your nerves and reduce anxiety.

Getting enough sleep is also important. Lack of sleep can exacerbate feelings of anxiety, so make sure you get enough sleep in the days leading up to the exam. This will help you feel more rested and relaxed on the day of the exam.

In addition to relaxation and sleep, it's important to stay positive. Instead of dwelling on negative thoughts, focus on positive affirmations and visualise yourself doing well on the exam. This can help to boost your confidence and reduce anxiety. If you can't help but dwell on negative thoughts, try to acknowledge them and understand where they are coming from. If you find yourself unable to move on from these thoughts, seek help from a friend, teacher, parent or school counsellor.

Lastly, being prepared is key. Make sure you prepare thoroughly for the exam so that you feel confident and in control. This might involve reviewing your notes, doing practice questions and seeking help from your teacher or tutor if needed. By being well prepared, you can feel more confident and less anxious on the day of the exam.

How to revise effectively

Revising for exams can help take away some of the stress – *and* you'll do better in the exam! Here are a few suggestions for effective exam revision:

1. **Use active revision techniques:** Rather than simply reading over your notes, actively engage with the material by testing yourself, summarising key points and applying what you've learned to practice questions.

2. **Focus on your weaknesses:** Spend more time revising topics that you find challenging.

3. **Use past papers:** Practising past exam papers can help you get a sense of what the exam will be like and identify areas that need more revision. Ask your teacher if there are past papers or example papers.

4. **Don't cram:** Cramming the night before the exam is unlikely to be effective. Instead, spread your revision out over several weeks or months leading up to the exam.

How to prepare for different types of exams

Exams can come in many shapes and sizes. Sometimes, you'll have an end-of-topic test or a practice exam during the term. At other times, you'll have more formal examinations. Here are some of the most common exams and some ways to approach them:

1. **Multiple choice exams:** Familiarise yourself with the structure of the exam and practise answering multiple choice questions. Pay attention to the wording of the questions and the possible answers.

2. **Essay exams:** Develop a clear and structured approach to answering essay questions. Practise writing essays under timed conditions and seek feedback from your teacher or tutor.

3. **Open-book exams:** Don't rely solely on your notes and textbooks. Use the open-book policy as an opportunity to apply what you've learned and demonstrate your understanding of the material.

4. **Practical exams:** Practise the practical tasks that will be assessed and make sure you understand the relevant theory. Familiarise yourself with the equipment and techniques that will be used during the exam.

NAPLAN exams

NAPLAN examinations are a test that students in Australia take every year to see how well they are doing in reading, writing, spelling, grammar and maths. It's important to remember that NAPLAN is not a test to see how smart or successful you are as an individual student; it's a test that helps teachers and schools understand how well the whole group is doing.

It's natural to feel a little bit nervous about taking a test, but it's important to remember that NAPLAN doesn't define you as a student or as a person. Your worth is not based on your test scores. You are unique, special and talented in your own way, and there are many things that you can do that a test can't measure.

If you're feeling stressed about NAPLAN, remember that you are not alone. It's okay to ask for help from your teachers or parents if you need it. There are also things that you can do to help you feel calmer and more confident, like getting enough sleep, eating well and taking breaks when you need them.

Most importantly, remember that NAPLAN is just one small part of your school experience. There are many other things that you will learn and achieve in school, like making friends, discovering your passions and having fun, so don't let NAPLAN stress you out or define you. Just do your best and remember that you are much more than a test score.

Chapter 7

Balancing academic and extracurricular activities

How to balance schoolwork and extracurricular activities

Balancing schoolwork and extracurricular activities can be a challenge. Here are some tips to help you balance academic and extracurricular activities:

- Make a schedule that includes time for homework, studying and extracurricular activities. This will help you manage your time more effectively and make sure you have enough time for everything.

- Keep track of assignments, deadlines and events using a planner or digital calendar. This will help you stay on top of your commitments and avoid procrastination.

- Let your teachers know about your extracurricular activities and ask for help or accommodations if needed. They may be able to give you extra time or provide additional resources to help you keep up with your schoolwork.

- Identify the activities that are most important to you and focus on those. It's okay to say no to activities that are not a priority.

- Learn to say no when you feel overwhelmed or overcommitted.

The benefits of extracurricular activities

Participating in extracurricular activities can provide a number of benefits that enhance your overall school experience. For example, extracurricular activities offer opportunities to develop new skills that are not typically taught in the classroom, such as leadership, teamwork and time management. These skills can be valuable not only in school but also in life beyond the classroom.

Another benefit of extracurricular activities is the opportunity to build relationships with your peers and develop a sense of community. By participating in extracurricular activities, you can connect with others who share your interests and build strong, lasting relationships. This sense of belonging can have a positive impact on your mental health and overall wellbeing.

Participating in extracurricular activities can also boost your confidence and self-esteem. When you excel in an activity or achieve a goal, you feel a sense of pride and accomplishment that can help you feel good about yourself. Extracurricular activities can improve your physical and mental health by providing opportunities for exercise and stress relief.

Taking part in extracurricular activities can provide a well-rounded and enriching school experience. By participating in activities that interest you, you can develop new skills, build relationships with your peers and boost your confidence and overall wellbeing.

How to prioritise and manage time

Managing time effectively is an important skill that can help you balance academic and extracurricular activities. Here are some steps to help you prioritise and manage your time:

- Identify your priorities and focus on those, cutting out other distractions.
- Create a schedule that includes time for homework, studying and extracurricular activities.
- Start assignments and projects as soon as possible to avoid feeling overwhelmed later on.
- Take regular breaks to avoid burnout and improve focus and productivity.
- Be prepared to adjust your schedule and priorities as needed to accommodate unexpected events or changes.

Managing your time with a matrix

A matrix is a kind of chart with different areas. You can use a matrix to help manage your time. Here's how:

1. Draw a square and divide it into four equal quadrants.

2. Label the quadrants as follows:
   - Urgent and important
   - Important but not urgent
   - Urgent but not important
   - Not urgent and not important.

3. Write down all of the tasks you need to complete in the appropriate quadrant based on their level of urgency and importance.

4. Start with the tasks in the **Urgent and important** quadrant, as these are the most critical tasks that require your immediate attention.

5. Next, move on to the **Important but not urgent** quadrant. These tasks are important for achieving your long-term goals and should be completed after the Urgent and important tasks are finished.

6. The **Urgent but not important** quadrant contains tasks that are not as critical, but still require your attention. Try to delegate or postpone these tasks if possible.

7. Finally, the **Not urgent and not important** quadrant contains tasks that are low priority and can be postponed or eliminated.

For example:

Urgent and important	Not urgent but important
• Submitting assignments on time • Studying for upcoming exams or quizzes • Attending class and arriving on time	• Developing good study habits and routines • Building positive relationships with teachers and peers • Participating in extracurricular activities or clubs
Urgent but not important	**Not urgent and not important**
• Responding to non-urgent emails or instant messages • Cleaning and organising your locker or desk (especially before your lunchbox starts to stink!) • Running errands or completing tasks for other people	• Watching TV or playing video games • Browsing social media or other non-educational websites • Engaging in non-educational activities during study time (procrastinating)

It's important to note that sometimes it's OK to do things from any of those quadrants – there's nothing wrong with watching TV *as long as* it doesn't interfere with the other parts of your life.

Ideally, you should focus a lot of your energy on the top right: not urgent but important. This is where you will develop skills you'll use your whole life.

How to balance short-term and long-term goals

Balancing short-term and long-term goals can be a challenge, but it's an important skill to develop. To balance short-term and long-term goals, it's important to set clear and achievable goals for both the short term and the long term. Short-term goals are those that can be achieved in the near future, while long-term goals may take several months or years to achieve.

Once you have identified your goals, it's important to prioritise them and focus on those that are most important to you. This can help you stay focused and avoid feeling overwhelmed by trying to achieve too many goals at once.

To achieve your goals, it's important to create a plan that outlines the steps you need to take to achieve them. This plan should include specific actions and deadlines to help you stay on track. Check out the chapter on setting goals for more information.

As you work towards your goals, it's important to stay motivated by tracking your progress and celebrating your achievements. Finally, it's important to be flexible and prepared to adjust your goals and plans as needed to accommodate unexpected events or changes. By being flexible and adaptable, you can stay on track towards achieving your goals, even in the face of challenges and setbacks.

Chapter 8

Understanding and managing stress

Understanding the causes of stress

Stress is a normal part of life and can be caused by a variety of factors. For students, common causes of stress can include academic pressure, peer pressure and life changes such as moving to a new school. Understanding what causes stress can help you manage it more effectively.

- **Academic pressure:** Academic stress can come from various sources, such as the pressure to perform well on tests or to keep up with the workload.

- **Peer pressure:** Peer pressure can be caused by the desire to fit in with a group, whether it's following a particular fashion trend or engaging in activities that you don't necessarily want to do.

- **Life changes:** Life changes, such as moving to a new school, adjusting to a new environment or dealing with family issues, can cause stress.

How to recognise and manage stress

Recognising the signs of stress is an important step in managing it. Common signs of stress include headaches, stomach-aches, trouble sleeping and feeling overwhelmed or anxious. Here are a few ways to manage stress:

- **Take a break:** Taking a break and doing something you enjoy can help you feel more relaxed and refreshed.

- **Practise relaxation techniques:** Techniques such as deep breathing, visualisation and progressive muscle relaxation can help you manage stress and anxiety. You can learn more about these in the following subtopic.

- **Seek support:** Talking to a trusted adult, such as a teacher or school counsellor, or a friend can help you manage stress and feel more supported.

Recognising and managing stress is an important part of maintaining your mental and physical wellbeing. By learning to recognise the signs of stress, practising relaxation techniques and seeking support when needed, you can manage stress and reduce its negative impact on your life.

Remember to take care of yourself by getting enough sleep, eating a healthy diet and engaging in regular physical activity. Effective time management can also help you prioritise and manage your tasks to reduce stress and avoid feeling overwhelmed.

How to relax and take care of yourself

Relaxation techniques can be a powerful way to manage stress. Here's a step-by-step guide to help you relax:

1. Find a quiet and comfortable place to sit or lie down.

2. Take slow, deep breaths, inhaling through your nose and exhaling through your mouth.

3. Visualise a calming scene, such as a beach or forest, and focus on the sounds, smells and sensations of the scene.

4. Try progressive muscle relaxation by tensing and then releasing each muscle group in your body, starting with your toes and working your way up to your head.

5. Engage in physical activity or hobbies that you enjoy, such as walking, dancing or drawing.

Taking time to relax and take care of yourself is crucial in managing stress and maintaining your mental and physical health. By engaging in relaxation techniques you can release stress and improve your overall wellbeing. Remember to take care of yourself and find what works best for you in managing stress.

How to prioritise and manage time to avoid stress

Effective time management can help you avoid feeling stressed and overwhelmed. Here are a few tips to help you prioritise and manage your time:

- **Create a schedule or to-do list:** Write down all the tasks you need to complete and allocate time for each one in a schedule or to-do list.

- **Break tasks into smaller, more manageable steps:** Breaking down larger tasks into smaller, more achievable steps can help you avoid feeling overwhelmed.

- **Set realistic goals:** Set achievable goals and be realistic about how much time you need to complete them.

- **Learn to say no:** Be willing to say no to commitments that may cause you to feel overwhelmed or stressed.

Here's an example of a to-do list for a typical day in secondary school:

- ✓ Check timetable in the morning.
- ✓ Pack everything I need for the day.
- ✓ Take extra snacks.
- ✓ Drink enough water!
- ✓ Join debate club in library at lunchtime.
- ✓ Bring home excursion form.
- ✓ Finish homework so tomorrow evening is free for basketball.

Chapter 9

Mental health matters: understanding and taking care of yourself

Signs and symptoms of mental health issues

Mental health is an important aspect of overall health and wellbeing, but it can be difficult to understand and identify. Mental health issues are common among young people, and it's important to be able to recognise the signs and symptoms.

One common sign of mental health issues is a change in mood. This may manifest as intense feelings of sadness, hopelessness or anxiety. You may also feel irritable or angry, even in situations that don't seem to warrant such strong emotions.

Changes in behaviour are also a common sign of mental health issues. You may find yourself withdrawing from social situations or avoiding activities that you used to enjoy. You may have trouble sleeping or find yourself oversleeping. Changes in appetite, such as overeating or undereating, are also common.

In addition to changes in mood and behaviour, mental health issues can also affect your thinking patterns. You may have trouble concentrating or making decisions, even about simple tasks. You may have negative or self-critical thoughts, and you may struggle to see things in a positive light.

It's important to understand the signs and symptoms of mental health issues so that you can identify when you or someone you know may need help. If you are experiencing any of these symptoms or if you are concerned about your mental health, it's important to seek help and support. Your school may have a counsellor or other mental health professional who can provide support and guidance, and there are many resources available online and in the community. Remember, mental health is just as important as physical health and seeking help is a sign of strength, not weakness.

Strategies and techniques for self-care and mental health

Self-care is an important part of maintaining your mental health and wellbeing. Here are a few strategies and techniques for self-care that can help you manage stress, anxiety and other mental health issues:

- **Exercise regularly:** Regular exercise can help reduce stress, improve mood and promote better sleep.

- **Practise mindfulness:** Mindfulness techniques such as deep breathing, meditation and yoga can help reduce anxiety and improve overall wellbeing.

- **Engage in creative activities:** Creative activities such as art, music or writing can be therapeutic and help you express yourself.

- **Build and maintain healthy relationships:** Positive social connections with family and friends can provide support and promote good mental health.

Resources and support for mental health

Mental health issues can be difficult to manage alone, and seeking support can be an important step in promoting mental health and wellbeing. There are many resources available to those who are struggling with mental health issues, including those listed below.

Your school may have a counsellor or other mental health professional who can provide support and guidance. School counsellors can offer a range of services, including individual and group counselling, referrals to community resources and support for mental health issues. They can also help students navigate academic and social challenges and can provide guidance on managing stress and other mental health concerns.

Helplines are another resource for those who are struggling with mental health issues. National or local helplines can provide information, support and resources for mental health issues. These helplines are staffed by trained professionals who can offer support and guidance on a range of mental health issues. They may also be able to provide referrals to local resources or mental health professionals.

In addition to in-person resources and helplines, there are also many online resources available for those who are struggling with mental health issues. Many websites and apps offer information and resources for mental health issues, including self-assessment tools, coping strategies and support forums. These resources can be helpful for those who are looking for support but may not feel comfortable seeking help in person.

No matter what resources you choose to use, it's important to remember that seeking help is a sign of strength, not weakness. Mental health issues are common and treatable, and there is no shame in seeking support and guidance. If you are struggling with mental health issues, reach out to the people and resources available to you and take the steps necessary to promote your own wellbeing.

Promoting positive attitudes towards mental health

Unfortunately, there can still be stigma and shame surrounding mental health issues. Promoting positive attitudes and breaking the stigma is important for helping people feel comfortable seeking help and support. Here are a few ways to promote positive attitudes towards mental health:

- **Educate yourself and others about mental health:** Learning more about mental health issues can help reduce stigma and promote understanding.

- **Be open about your own experiences:** Sharing your own experiences with mental health issues can help reduce stigma and encourage others to seek help. Only share what you are comfortable with.

- **Encourage others to seek help:** Encouraging others to seek help and offering support can help reduce stigma and promote positive attitudes towards mental health.

Chapter 10

Being yourself: embracing your unique identity

How to be true to yourself

It can be tough to stay true to yourself when there is so much pressure to fit in with peers and societal norms. Here are a few tips to help you be true to yourself:

- **Take time for self-reflection:** Spend some time thinking about what you enjoy doing and what makes you happy.
- **Identify your values:** Understanding what is important to you can help you make decisions that align with your beliefs.
- **Be honest with yourself:** Don't try to be someone you're not just to impress others.
- **Follow your passions:** Pursue the things you love, even if they are not popular or mainstream.
- **Surround yourself with positive people:** Find people who accept you for who you are and support you in your interests and passions.

Here are a couple of easy activities you could try:

1. Write down three things that make you unique and special. Share them with a friend or family member and celebrate your individuality.
2. Write down three things you value. These could be things like friendship, family, truth, justice and so on. You don't have to share these, but you could check on them every now and again to see if your thoughts have shifted over time.

How to deal with peer pressure

Peer pressure can be a challenging experience, especially when it involves doing things that go against your beliefs and values. However, it is important to learn how to handle peer pressure and stand up for what you believe in. Here are some tips on how to deal with peer pressure:

- **Be confident in your decisions:** Trust your gut feeling and the choices you make. Believe in your choices and don't feel guilty or ashamed about them.

- **Find like-minded friends:** Try to make friends with people who share your interests and values. Surrounding yourself with friends who respect and appreciate you for who you are will make it easier to avoid peer pressure.

- **Learn to say no:** It's important to learn to say no when you don't feel comfortable doing something. You don't have to agree with everything your friends do or say, and it's okay to decline an invitation or activity that goes against your beliefs.

- **Seek support from an adult:** Talking to a trusted adult, such as a teacher, school counsellor or parent, can be helpful when dealing with peer pressure. They can provide support, guidance and advice on how to handle difficult situations.

- **Remember that it's okay to be different:** Embrace your unique qualities and don't let others pressure you to change. Everyone is different; it's what makes us unique and special. You should be proud of who you are and not let others make you feel inferior.

How to build self-confidence and self-esteem

Having self-confidence and a positive self-image can help you be true to yourself and embrace your unique identity. Here are a few ways to build self-confidence and self-esteem:

- **Practise positive self-talk:** Replace negative thoughts with positive affirmations.

- **Celebrate your accomplishments:** Recognise your successes, no matter how small they may seem.

- **Step out of your comfort zone:** Challenge yourself to try new things and take on new experiences.

- **Be kind to yourself:** Treat yourself with the same kindness and respect that you show to others.

Try this activity: make a list of five things you are good at and five things you would like to improve on. Practise being kind to yourself by focusing on your strengths and setting realistic goals for improvement. We'll talk more about setting goals in the next chapter.

How to embrace your unique identity

Celebrating your unique qualities is an important part of being true to yourself. Here are a few tips for embracing your unique identity:

- **Recognise that everyone is different:** It's okay to be unique; it's what makes you special.

- **Be proud of your background and heritage:** Your family history and culture are an important part of who you are.

- **Try new things:** Explore new hobbies and interests to learn more about yourself and what you enjoy.

- **Embrace your personal style:** Dress in a way that makes you feel comfortable and confident.

- **Stand up for yourself:** Don't let others put you down or make you feel like you need to change.

Chapter 11

Looking to the future: setting goals and dreaming big

How to set goals and plan for the future

As you get ready to start secondary school, it's important to start thinking about your future and the goals you want to achieve. Here are some tips to help you set goals, overcome obstacles and achieve success:

- **Set SMART goals:** SMART stands for specific, measurable, achievable, relevant and time-bound. Make sure your goals meet each of these criteria.

- **Make a plan:** Break your goals down into smaller, manageable steps. Create a plan to help you achieve each step.

- **Track your progress:** Keep track of your progress and celebrate your achievements along the way.

- **Get support:** Talk to your teachers, parents or mentors for guidance and support.

Here's an example of a SMART goal for a secondary student:

- **Specific:** I want to improve my maths grade from a B to an A.

- **Measurable:** I will measure my progress by tracking my grades on each maths assignment and test.

- **Achievable:** I will achieve this goal by attending after-school tutoring twice a week, completing all homework assignments and studying for each maths test.

- **Relevant:** Improving my maths grade is important for my academic success and my future goals.

- **Time-bound:** I will achieve this goal by the end of the semester.

How to overcome obstacles and achieve success

Staying focused on your goals is essential to achieving success. Here are some tips to help you stay focused and motivated:

- **Keep your goals in mind:** Make sure your goals are specific and measurable. Write them down and keep them somewhere visible so you can be reminded of them every day.

- **Develop resilience:** Embrace challenges and view them as opportunities to learn and grow.

- **Act:** Break your goals down into smaller, manageable steps. Take small steps towards your goals every day. This will help you avoid feeling overwhelmed and make it easier to stay motivated.

- **Persevere:** Don't give up when things get tough. Remember that challenges are part of the learning process and you can overcome them with hard work and dedication.

Here's an activity to help you stay focused on your goals:

1. Choose a SMART goal you want to achieve, such as improving your grades in a particular subject or learning a new skill.
2. Write down your goal and break it down into smaller steps.
3. Create a visual reminder of your goal, such as a vision board or a post-it note.
4. Every day, take a small step towards your goal, such as reading a chapter in a book or practising a new skill for 10 minutes.
5. Celebrate your successes along the way and remind yourself of your progress.

Remember, staying focused on your goals is a key component of achieving success. By developing resilience, taking action and persevering, you can overcome obstacles and achieve great things in your life.

How to think big and dream big

When it comes to thinking big and dreaming big, there are several steps you can take to help guide your journey. Here are a few tips to get you started:

1. **Identify your passions and interests:** What makes you happy and fulfilled? What do you enjoy doing in your free time? Use these passions and interests to guide your goals and aspirations. This will make it easier to stay motivated and focused on what truly matters to you.

2. **Visualise your future:** Take some time to imagine what your ideal future looks like. What kind of career do you want? Where do you want to live? What kind of lifestyle do you envision for yourself? Once you have a clear picture in your mind, set goals to help you achieve it.

3. **Don't limit yourself:** It's easy to fall into the trap of thinking small and setting goals that are easily achievable. But if you really want to think big and dream big, don't be afraid to aim high. Set goals that may seem out of reach but are still attainable with hard work and dedication.

Remember, thinking big and dreaming big is about setting your sights high and believing in yourself. By identifying your passions and interests, visualising your future and not limiting yourself, you can achieve great things and make your dreams a reality.

How to stay motivated and focused

Staying motivated and focused is an important aspect of achieving your goals. Here are a few tips to help you stay on track:

1. Remind yourself of your goals daily by keeping them in sight. Write them down and put them in a visible place, such as on a wall or mirror. This will help you to stay focused on what you want to achieve.

2. Taking breaks is important to avoid burnout and stay motivated. Take short breaks throughout the day to rest and recharge. This will help you to maintain your energy and focus.

3. Staying organised is key to staying on track. Keep a schedule or planner to help you stay organised and prioritise your tasks. This will help you to manage your time effectively and reduce stress.

4. Finally, celebrate your successes. Acknowledging your achievements can help you to stay motivated and focused. Celebrate even small accomplishments, such as finishing a project or meeting a deadline. This will help you to maintain a positive mindset and stay motivated to achieve your goals.

Chapter 12

Devices and digital technologies

Setting healthy boundaries for device use

As you move into secondary school, it is likely that you will be using digital devices, including laptops and tablets, more often. To get the most out of the beneficial aspects of technology, it is important to set boundaries around how you use devices. Here are a few ways you can set healthy boundaries:

- Use your device's built-in features to disable notifications early in the morning and towards bedtime.

- Turn off devices at night and put them on charge in a different room.

- Set time limits on potentially addictive apps, such as games or social media.

- Establish designated screen-free times or locations, such as no screens during meals or in the bedroom.

- Use tools such as screen-time tracking apps or social media filters to help manage your device use.

- Take breaks to stretch and move around, especially if you have been using a device for an extended period.

- Consider limiting your device use to specific times or tasks, rather than constantly checking your device throughout the day.

- Remember to prioritise face-to-face communication and interactions with others, rather than relying solely on digital communication.

By setting boundaries around your device use, you can ensure that you are using technology in a healthy and balanced way. It's important to find a balance that works for you and your lifestyle and to be mindful of the potential negative impacts of excessive device use.

The impact of device use on mental health

Using devices too much can also affect your mental health, which is just as important as your physical health. Mental health issues can be harder to recognise than physical health problems because they are not always visible. For example, it's easy to see how poor posture while using a device can lead to neck pain, but it's harder to see the connection between using devices a lot and feeling lonely or depressed.

Here are some of the possible negative effects of device use on mental health:

- **Depression:** Depression is a mental health condition characterised by feelings of sadness, hopelessness and lack of interest in activities that a person usually enjoys. Prolonged use of devices, such as smartphones or laptops, can contribute to feelings of depression by reducing face-to-face social interactions, which can lead to feelings of loneliness and isolation.

- **Difficulty regulating emotions:** Devices can also disrupt a person's ability to regulate their emotions. For example, constantly checking social media or receiving notifications can cause a person to feel anxious or stressed, as they may feel pressure to constantly be connected and responsive.

- **Loneliness:** Spending excessive amounts of time on devices can also contribute to feelings of loneliness. Research has shown that people who spend more time on social media are more likely to report feeling lonely, as they may compare their own lives to the carefully curated and often idealised versions of other people's lives that they see online.

- **Anxiety:** Constant device use can also lead to feelings of anxiety, as people may feel pressure to be constantly connected and responsive to notifications and messages. This can lead to a feeling of being overwhelmed and a difficulty in disconnecting from work or social obligations.

- **Addiction:** It is possible for people to become addicted to their devices in the same way that they might become addicted to other behaviours, such as gambling or using drugs. This can lead to negative consequences, such as difficulty concentrating, difficulty sleeping and problems with relationships and work.

It's important to remember that these are just some of the potential negative effects of device use and that not everyone who uses devices will experience these problems. However, it is important to be aware of the potential risks and to find a balance in device use.

Strategies for reducing device addiction

If you find that your device use is impacting your physical or mental health, there are some strategies you can try to reduce device addiction and get back to face-to-face interactions.

- **Take breaks from social media:** If you find you're spending lots of time on social media, consider taking regular breaks. This can help reduce feelings of FOMO (fear of missing out) and give you a chance to engage in other activities.

- **Make time for face-to-face interactions:** Try to spend time with friends and family in person, rather than just communicating with them through devices. This could mean going out for meals or activities or simply spending time together at home.

- **Find other ways to relax and unwind:** Consider finding other ways to relax and unwind that don't involve using devices, like going for a walk, reading a book or engaging in a hobby.

- **Seek support:** If you're having difficulty reducing your device use or are struggling with feelings of addiction, it can be helpful to seek support from a trusted friend, family member or healthcare professional. They can provide guidance and help you develop strategies for finding a healthier balance.

The potential benefits of digital detoxing

A digital detox is a way to take a break from devices and disconnect from the internet. This can be a helpful strategy for reducing device addiction and increasing face-to-face interactions. To complete a digital detox, you can turn off your devices and make a pledge to stay offline for a certain amount of time, such as a day, a weekend or even a week. This can be challenging, especially if you are used to being online a lot, but it can also be very rewarding.

During a digital detox, you can focus on other activities and hobbies, spend time with friends and family in person, or simply relax and unwind. You might find that you feel more present and mindful when you are not constantly checking your phone or scrolling through social media. You might also notice that you feel more relaxed and less anxious without the constant notifications and alerts.

If you are considering a digital detox, it can be helpful to plan and arrange with friends and family to support you. You might also want to set some goals for your detox, such as spending more time exercising, reading or engaging in a creative hobby. It can also be helpful to enlist the support of a trusted friend, family member or healthcare professional to help you stay on track and find a healthier balance with your device use.

Chapter 13

Growing and learning: how to embrace change

Understanding the importance of change

Change is a normal part of life, and it's important to understand why it's necessary. Change can help us to learn new things, grow as individuals and achieve our goals. Whether it's starting a new school or trying out a new activity, change can be scary, but it can also be exciting.

When we embrace change, we open ourselves up to new experiences and opportunities. We may discover new talents or interests, make new friends or learn new skills. By embracing change, we can develop resilience and adaptability, which are important life skills that will serve us well in the future.

How to adapt to new situations

Here are five approaches that may help you to adapt to new situations:

1. **Stay positive:** Keep a positive attitude and remember that change can be an opportunity for growth and learning.

2. **Be flexible:** Try new things and step out of your comfort zone.

3. **Take things one step at a time:** Focus on the present moment and don't worry about what's to come.

4. **Take breaks:** If you feel overwhelmed, take a break and do something that relaxes you.

5. **Ask for help:** Don't be afraid to ask for help if you need it. Talk to your teachers, friends or family if you're struggling to adapt to a new situation.

Adapting to new situations can be challenging, but it's an important skill to develop. By staying positive, being flexible and focusing on the present moment, you can navigate change with confidence and ease. Remember that change is a natural part of life that can bring new opportunities and experiences you may not have imagined before. Embrace change and keep growing and learning!

How to grow and learn from failure

Resilience is the ability to bounce back from difficult situations and to keep moving forward. Being resilient means being able to face challenges and adversity with courage, confidence and a positive attitude. Resilience is an important skill to have, especially when facing new challenges and changes.

To develop resilience, it's important to build a support system of family, friends and mentors who can offer encouragement and advice. Surround yourself with positive people who will lift you up and help you stay motivated.

Remember to take care of yourself by getting enough sleep, eating healthy foods and getting regular exercise. These habits can help you feel more energised and focused, which can help you stay resilient in the face of challenges.

Practise mindfulness and other relaxation techniques, such as deep breathing or meditation. These practices can help you stay calm and centred when facing stressful situations.

Finally, remember that resilience takes time and practice to develop. Don't give up if you face setbacks or challenges along the way. Instead, view them as opportunities to learn and grow, and keep moving forward with a positive attitude.

How to embrace change and uncertainty

Change and uncertainty can be scary, but they can also be opportunities for growth and learning. Embracing change and uncertainty means staying positive and open-minded. Remember that change can lead to new experiences and opportunities.

Try to focus on the things you can control, like your attitude and how you respond to change. Take things one step at a time, and don't be afraid to ask for help if you need it.

It's also important to take care of yourself during times of change and uncertainty. Make time for activities that relax you and make you happy, like spending time with friends or practising a hobby. Remember that change is a normal part of life, and with time and practice it will become easier to embrace.

Conclusion

Conclusion

Congratulations – you made it! If you've read this far, hopefully you'll be feeling well prepared for the transition to secondary school. As you get ready for this exciting new chapter in your life, it's important to remember that you have the power to shape your own experience. By using the tips, strategies and advice in this book, you can take proactive steps to prepare for the transition, build your confidence and resilience, and navigate the ups and downs of this exciting new adventure.

Throughout this book, we've covered a wide range of topics that are important for young people transitioning to secondary school. We've talked about the importance of setting goals, managing expectations, building a support network, making friends, navigating the classroom and homework, dealing with bullies, finding your passion, managing stress and mental health, and much more.

But beyond these specific topics, there are a few key takeaways that we hope you'll keep in mind as you embark on this new journey. Here are a few final thoughts to keep in mind:

- First, be proactive in your preparation. Use the tips and strategies in this book to start thinking about your goals, your support network, your time management and your mental health. Don't wait until you're in the thick of things to start thinking about these important issues.

- Second, be kind to yourself. Remember that transitioning to secondary school is a big change, and it's normal to feel a range of emotions. It's okay to feel nervous, scared or uncertain at times. Be kind to yourself and give yourself the space and support you need to adapt to this new environment.

- Third, be open-minded and flexible. Embrace change and uncertainty, and be willing to try new things. You never know what new experiences and opportunities may come your way if you're open to them.

- Fourth, stay true to yourself. Don't compromise your values, beliefs or interests in order to fit in or please others. Be confident in who you are, and embrace your unique identity.

- Finally, remember that you are not alone. You have a whole community of people – your friends, family, teachers and mentors – who are here to support you and help you succeed. Don't hesitate to reach out to them for help, advice or just a listening ear.

I hope this book has been helpful and informative as you prepare for the transition to secondary school. Remember, this is just the beginning of an exciting new journey filled with endless possibilities and opportunities for growth and learning. With the right mindset and the right support, you can make the most of this experience and build a bright future for yourself.

Good luck!

The High School Success Series

Student Wellbeing Handbook: How to Thrive and Be Your Best Self
Author: Leon Furze

Starting High School: Confidently Navigate the School Experience
Author: Leon Furze

Foundational Study Skills for High School Students: Unlocking the 8 Superhabits of Study
Author: Scott Francis

Study Skills for Ambitious Senior Students: The High-Performance Advantage of the 8 Superhabits of Study
Author: Scott Francis

Reading Skills Handbook: Unlocking Successful Reading Strategies
Author: Ben White

Writing Skills Handbook: Acquiring High-Performance Writing Techniques
Author: Ben White

Grammar Skills Handbook: Mastering Grammar and Punctuation
Authors: Rod Campbell & Graham Ryles

Financial Literacy Handbook: Money Skills for High School and Beyond
Author: Scott Francis

www.ingramcontent.com/pod-product-compliance
Lightning Source LLC
Chambersburg PA
CBHW050308120526
44590CB00016B/2538